Guided journal to help you keep that connection as you begin to find your place in this world without your father being here in the physical.

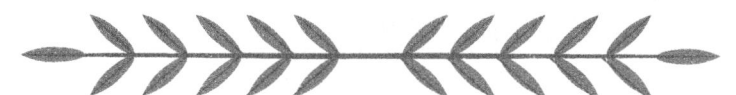

I will always have you in
my heart.
I love you Dad.

From:

_____

You & Me

My First Memory Of You

Our First Trip Together

Our Inside Jokes

Craziest thing we did together

Our favorite place

First Give You Gave Me

Life Skills I'm Glad You Tought Me

Our Favorite Movies

Today, I really miss

If I could go back in time I would do this differently

I don't ever want to forget...

When I think of you I feel...

On fathers day, I remember you by doing this...

Our favorite songs

The day you died

Printed in Great Britain
by Amazon